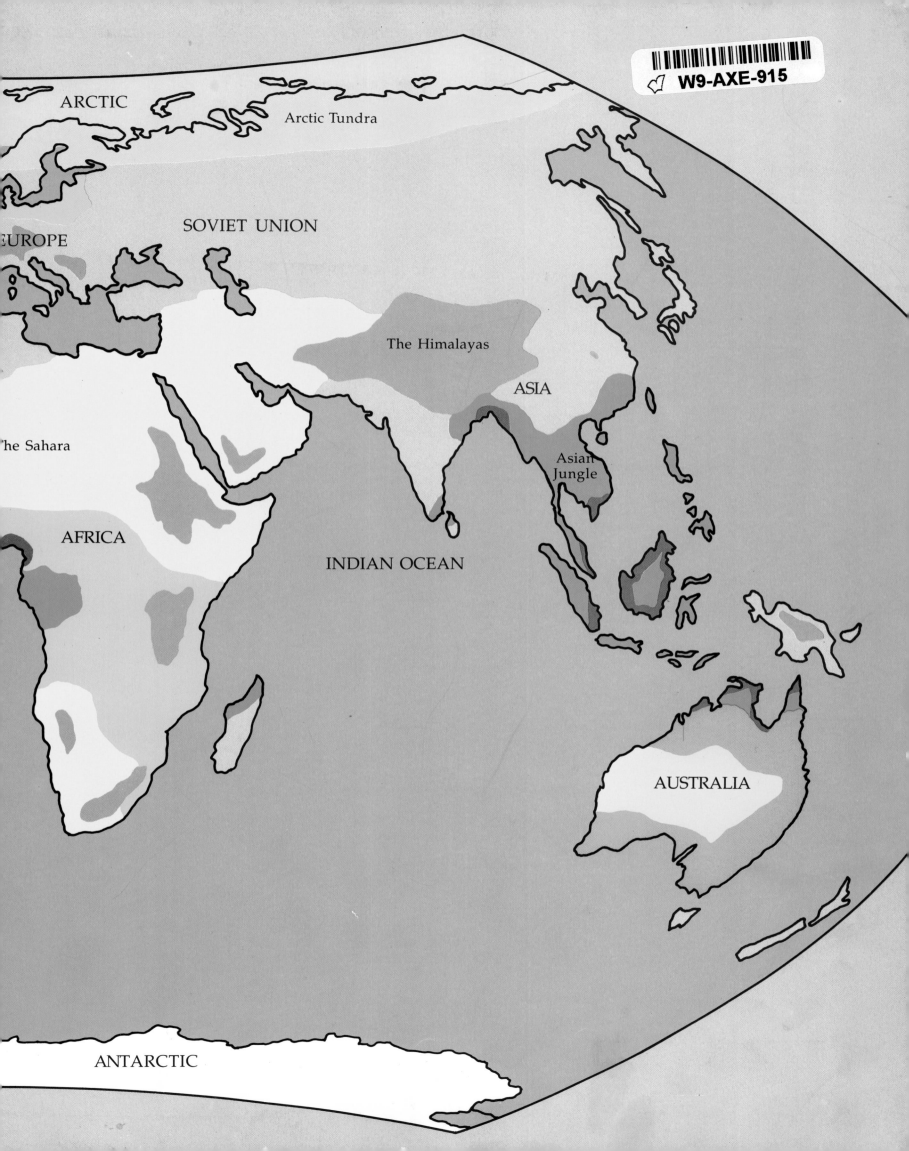

ARCTIC

Arctic Tundra

SOVIET UNION

EUROPE

The Himalayas

ASIA

The Sahara

Asian
Jungle

AFRICA

INDIAN OCEAN

AUSTRALIA

ANTARCTIC

Andrew Bale would like to thank
Barbara Wells for kindly allowing him
to draw her captive bred lanner falcon.

Text copyright © 1991 by Jenny Wood
Illustrations copyright © 1991 by Andrew Bale

Macmillan Publishing Company is part of the
Maxwell Communication Group of Companies.

Macmillan Publishing Company
866 Third Avenue
New York, NY 10022

First published by Kingfisher Books, London, England.

First American edition

Printed in Singapore

10 9 8 7 6 5 4 32 1

Library of Congress Cataloging-in -Publication Data
Wood, Jenny.
The animal kingdom / Jenny Wood ; illustrated by Andrew Bale. —
1st American ed.
  p. cm.
Summary: Describes such animal habitats as tundra, swamps,
deserts, jungle, and sea, briefly introducing some of the animals
that live in them.
ISBN 0-02-793395-4
1. Animals—Juvenile literature. 2. Habitat (Ecology)—Juvenile
literature. [1. Animals—Habitat.] I. Bale, Andrew, ill. II. Title.
QL49.W695 1991   591.5'26—dc20   91-14567

THE ANIMAL KINGDOM

Written by
JENNY WOOD

Illustrated by
ANDREW BALE

Macmillan Publishing Company
New York

Maxwell Macmillan International
New York   Oxford   Singapore   Sydney

CONTENTS

The giant panda lives in remote parts
of China where its favorite food,
bamboo, grows. Unfortunately,
like some of the other animals you
will read about in this book, pandas
are in danger of dying out. That is
why they have become the symbol
of the World Wildlife Fund—
an organization that tries to protect
endangered animals, plants,
and their habitats.

The Arctic

At the top of the world lies an area of frozen ocean surrounded mainly by land. This is the Arctic. Most of the animals here have thick coats of fur or a layer of fat under their skins to protect them from the cold. Some Arctic animals hibernate, sleeping through the winter. Others live there only during the short summer, when the days are longer and there is more food.

Polar bears like to eat seals.
They wait by a breathing hole
in the ice until a seal comes up for air.
Then they pounce.

Puffins nest
in burrows
on the tops
of steep cliffs.
During the summer,
when all Arctic animals breed,
the colors on a puffin's beak
become brighter.

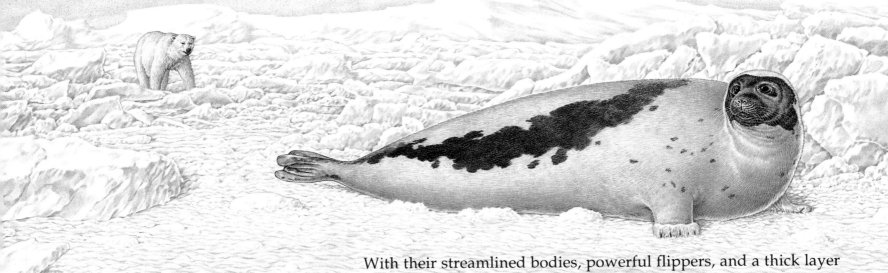

With their streamlined bodies, powerful flippers, and a thick layer of fat under their skin, seals are well suited to life in Arctic waters.

Seals cannot breathe under water.
When the sea is frozen over, they find holes
in the ice through which to breathe.

Walruses use their tusks to pull themselves out of the water and as weapons when fighting enemies, such as sharks and killer whales.

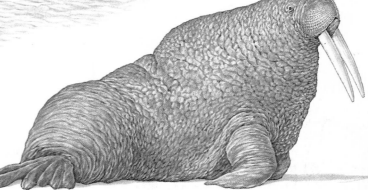

Arctic Tundra

The Arctic tundra is a frozen wilderness stretching across the northern edges of Canada, Europe and Asia. Only small plants, growing mainly in sheltered spots, can survive the bitter wind and cold.

In winter some animals move into the forests further south, where it is warmer and food is plentiful. Others hibernate in tunnels beneath the snow. In summer the sun rarely sets. The snow melts, plants bloom, and many animals travel long distances to breed here.

Arctic terns visit the tundra in summer to breed. In winter they fly south to the Antarctic, spending many months of each year in the air.

A pack of wolves can attack and kill a caribou which is much larger than themselves.

The stoat's fur changes from reddish-brown to white in winter. Its name changes too, and it is then called an ermine. Only the black tip of its tail remains the same color all year round.

The snowy owl has feathers right down to its toes. A soft layer of down next to its skin keeps it warm, and oily outer feathers keep it dry.

The Arctic fox will eat almost anything and often travels far in search of food. In winter its coat turns white to blend in with the snowy landscape. This way, it can hunt without being seen by its prey.

The musk ox has very, very long hair.
A heavy layer of wool underneath its hair
helps to keep out the cold.

In summer caribou wander
across the tundra feeding
on grass and plants. They eat
as much as they can. During
the winter, when food is hard
to find, they live off the fat
stored in their bodies.

Baby caribou can walk
when only an hour old.
This is important because
they have to be ready
to travel with the herd,
which keeps moving
all year round.

Temperate Forests

In summer a temperate forest is lush and green. But as autumn sets in, the leaves change to brilliant shades of red and gold and start to fall. By winter the bare branches are often covered with snow. The forest then becomes quieter. Some animals hibernate, and many forest birds fly south to find a warmer winter home.

In North America's temperate forests, there are ponds and lakes and rivers hidden among the trees. Some of the animals there can live both on land and in water. Today these forests are a lot smaller than they once were. People have felled so many trees that much of the wildlife is now in danger.

Beavers have such strong teeth that they can gnaw right through a tree trunk! Once the tree has fallen, they cut it up and use the wood to build dams. These dams are built across rivers to make ponds. The beavers build mud and stick homes, called lodges, in the middle of the pond.

A moose spends most of each summer
wading through streams and lakes,
looking for water plants to eat.
In winter it nibbles the bark
and branches of young trees.

As soon as an osprey sees a fish,
it dives from the sky and, quick
as a flash, grabs the slippery prey
with its sharp talons.

Black bears love honey. They climb trees
and scoop it from bees' nests. Although
the bear's snout is very sensitive,
its thick fur helps to protect the rest
of its body from bee stings.

Porcupines eat buds, twigs, and bark.
They scrape the bark from tree trunks
with their sharp claws.
When threatened, a porcupine
raises the sharp bristles of hair,
called quills, on its body.

Any creature that frightens or tries
to attack a skunk is in for a shock.
The skunk will squirt a jet
of nasty smelling liquid at the intruder's
eyes, blinding it for a short time.

13

Mountains

The scenery and climate change from one level of a mountain to another. Right at the top are snow-covered peaks. Here animals cannot survive the bitter cold and lack of food. Below the peaks lie rocky cliffs and crags where wild sheep and goats live, eating shrubs and tufts of grass. Many birds nest here, too. On the lower grassy slopes animals, such as yaks, graze. As the seasons change, many mountain animals move from one level to another to find food.

The world's highest mountain range on land is the Himalayan range in Asia. The Himalayas separate northern India from China.

Wild yaks are huge heavy animals.
They can walk and climb great distances.

Domestic yaks are smaller and gentler than wild yaks.
The people of the Himalayas use domestic yaks
to carry goods across the mountains.
These animals also provide
milk and meat, and their hair
is used to make cloth.
Even their dung is used as fuel.

The pale color of the snow leopard's coat helps it
creep unnoticed over the snow in search of birds, sheep,
and goats. Its summer home is high up in the mountains.
In winter it comes down into the lower valleys.

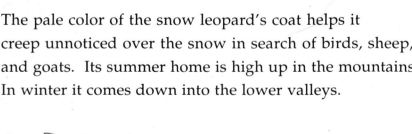

Pikas are related to the rabbit family. They live in groups
among loose rocks on the mountainsides, and spend most
of their time collecting food. When in danger,
pikas give loud squeaking calls to warn each other.

Swifts are strong, fast fliers. They can stay in the air for many hours and can catch insects while in flight. The swifts of Nepal fly at heights of over 20,000 ft (6,000 m).

The Asian ibex is a type of wild goat. It is very sure-footed, and can stand on a peak just big enough for its four feet.

15

Swamps

Swamps are areas that are always wet. They can be salt or fresh water. Many plants, animals, fish and birds thrive in the dampness of a swamp.

The Everglades is a huge tropical swamp in Florida. It is like a slow moving river, flowing to the sea. At one end, the swamp is fresh water, covered with a coarse grass called saw grass. Nearer the sea, the swamp is salty. Thick forests of trees called black mangroves grow there. The roots of these trees are unusual. They grow where they will be uncovered at low tide because they need to breathe.

Waterlily flowers grow on long stalks that rise up from the muddy bottom of the swamp. Some waterlilies bloom during the day, others at night.

The American alligator lives in the swampy grass. It swims by sweeping its tail from side to side. The female alligator lays her eggs in a grassy nest. She then covers them with more grass and other plants. When the young hatch, they make high-pitched squeaking sounds. The mother quickly scratches open the nest to set them free.

The anhinga is also known as the snakebird, because it often swims underwater with only its head and snakelike neck above the surface.

The gar pike eats other fish.
Its beak has large, sharp teeth.

When looking for food, the great blue heron stands perfectly still in the water. As soon as it sees a fish, frog, or other small animal, it moves swiftly and seizes the victim in its long bill.

The water moccasin's bite can be deadly.
This poisonous snake is also known as the cottonmouth, because when under attack it throws back its head and opens its white-lined mouth wide as a warning signal.

The bobcat is a wild cat. It usually hunts at night, looking for rabbits, birds, mice, rats and squirrels. Bobcats are good swimmers.

Deserts

Some deserts are hot all year round; others are cold in winter, but all are very, very dry. Years can go by without a drop of rain!

The Sahara, in northern Africa, is the largest hot desert in the world. Parts of it are sandy, but there are areas of rock, too.

During the day, it is extremely hot, but at night it is very cold. These sudden changes in temperature, as well as the lack of water, make life hard for all living things.

In parts of the desert, water from under the ground reaches the surface. In such places many plants, including trees, can grow all year round. These fertile areas are called oases.

Addax antelopes were once found all over the Sahara, but now there are only a few left. They hardly ever drink. Instead, they get most of the water they need from the plants they eat.

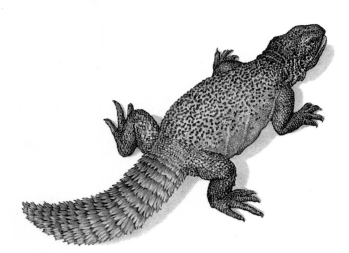

Many reptiles, such as spiny-tailed lizards, are well suited to desert life, needing very little food and water to survive.

During the day, the fennec fox shelters in burrows from the heat of the sun. At night, when it is out hunting for small animals and birds, its furry coat keeps it warm.

The camel can travel across the desert for days or weeks
without having to drink and gets water from its food.
The fat stored in its hump provides some of the energy it needs.
Its wide, padded feet prevent it from sinking into the soft sand.

During twilight, the lanner falcon
soars over the sand,
hunting for small animals.

The desert sidewinding viper buries itself
in the sand and lies in wait for rodents and lizards.
When prey comes within reach, the viper
darts forward in a spray of sand and bites
its victim with its poisonous fangs.

Jerboas are usually sandy colored and blend in well
with their surroundings. This is a useful camouflage
against predators.

South American Jungle

Jungles are found in the hot, wet parts of the world where it rains nearly every day. The heat and dampness help trees and plants reach spectacular heights. The biggest jungle of all is in South America, where the Amazon River flows. Millions of different animals, birds, and insects live there—either high up in the sunlit treetops, down below in the river, or on the dark, dank jungle floor.

Most hummingbirds are tiny. One species is no bigger than a bumblebee! They are called hummingbirds because of the humming sound made by the rapid beating of their wings.

The anaconda is the biggest snake in the world. It usually lives along the riverbank. It can swim as well as climb.

South American monkeys such as the spider monkey can hang from tree branches by their tails.

Toucans usually live in large, noisy groups. They eat fruit and berries.

A howler monkey's call can be heard almost two miles away.

Jaguars hide during the day and prowl around at night, hunting for rodents and deer.

The three-toed sloth spends most of its life hanging upside-down from the branch of a tree. Its strong hooklike claws help to give it a good grip.

Asian Jungle

Jungle trees grow leaves all year round. The top
leaves form such a thick roof over the whole jungle
that very little light or wind reaches the ground below.
Shade-loving plants grow beneath the tallest trees,
and climbing plants called lianas twist around the trunks
and branches. Flowering plants grow from the tree
branches, to be as near the sunlight as possible.

Many Asian jungle animals begin to stir as night falls.
By searching for food in the dark, they run less risk
of being noticed by their prey or of becoming prey themselves.

An orangutan sleeps in a simple nest
of twigs and branches that it builds
in the fork of a tree. It moves around
the jungle and builds a new nest each night.

With their keen senses of smell
and hearing, tapirs have little trouble getting around in the dark.
By twisting and turning their sensitive snouts, they can easily
find the leaves and grasses they eat.

The rafflesia is the largest flower in the world.
It has no leaves and no stem, and looks
and smells like rotting meat.

Flying foxes are not foxes at all
but bats with foxlike heads.
They roost by day and, at night
fly off in groups, looking for
flowers and ripening fruit to eat.

Tarsiers wait until sunset
before hunting for small lizards
and insects to eat. They are
very agile, and can leap
from tree to tree in
the pitch dark
without falling.

The Sumatran tiger
usually hunts under cover
of night. It steals up on its prey
and suddenly leaps forward, stunning the animal
with a mighty blow from one of its front paws.
The tiger then bites and squeezes the animal's throat
until it is dead. If the tiger cannot eat the whole animal,
it hides the carcass and returns whenever it is hungry.

Tropical Grasslands

Tropical grasslands cover huge areas of Africa,
and smaller areas of Australia, India, and
South America. In Africa they are called savannahs.
In Australia they are called downlands,
and in South America they are called pampas.
For most of the year they are hot, dry places.

Tropical grasses have long roots.
They are not damaged by grazing,
and send up new shoots as soon as
the rainy season begins.

Africa's savannahs are home to millions of grazing
animals, which live in huge herds. Unfortunately,
large numbers of these animals have been killed by humans,
and farms and towns have been built where they once
roamed free. Today many of them live in national parks
where hunting is forbidden. Others are still in danger.

There are several different
types of zebra. Each has
its own pattern of stripes.
Zebras nibble each other
to keep their skins
free from insects.

The cheetah is the fastest land mammal.
It can sprint at a top speed of about 70 mph
(112 km/h), but only for a short time,
because it gets tired quickly.

The ostrich is the world's largest bird.
It cannot fly, but it can run at speeds
of up to 30 mph (48km/h).

Lions live in groups called prides. They spend most
of each day resting. At night the females usually hunt
for food while one or two adults watch over the cubs.

Where there are trees, elephants and giraffes
munch the leaves and shoots.
To keep up their strength, elephants spend
about 18 hours each day feeding.
Giraffes usually have no trouble finding food.
Unlike many other animals, they can reach
leaves at the top of trees.

The white rhinoceros is one
of the rarest African mammals.
It usually grazes alone.

Vultures can spot food
from high up in the sky.
They look out for the flesh
of dead animals, called carrion.
As soon as one vulture
swoops down, others follow.
Sometimes they eat so much,
they are too heavy to fly away.

Australia

Australia is a huge island in the Pacific Ocean. Much of the land is desert or dry grassland, so most people live near the coast where there is more rain.

Millions of years ago, all the world's continents formed one huge land mass. Gradually this land mass broke up and Australia became an island. Because of this, many Australian animals are very different from animals that live in other parts of the world. A lot of them are marsupials. This means that the mothers carry their babies in pouches on their stomachs.

Koalas are marsupials. They spend most of their time in the branches of eucalyptus trees which they grip tightly with their sharp, curved claws and long toes.
Koalas sleep for most of the day and feed at night.

Cockatoos often fly in large, noisy flocks. They eat seeds, nuts, and fruit.

Platypuses live in burrows along riverbanks. They feed on snails, insects, and small shellfish which they scoop up with their ducklike bills. The platypus is a very unusual mammal. It lays eggs instead of giving birth to live babies.

The sugar glider is a "flying" marsupial. It has flaps of furred skin between its front and back legs. These flaps stretch out and allow it to glide between treetops. Sugar gliders eat insects, nectar, pollen, and tree sap.

Emus cannot fly but they can run fast. The mother lays the eggs and then the father sits on them until they are ready to hatch.

Kangaroos move by jumping forward on their strong back legs. Their tails help them balance as they leap through the air. When a baby kangaroo, called a joey, is born, it crawls into a pouch on its mother's stomach. It stays there for over eight months until fully developed.

The frilled lizard often runs on its back legs to keep its body away from the hot ground. It scares off enemies by spreading out its neck frill.

The Sea

Almost three-quarters of the Earth's surface is covered by sea.
Underwater lie the world's greatest mountain ranges,
canyons, volcanoes, sand dunes and wide, empty plains.
   Every level of the sea has some form of life in it.
Most marine animals and plants live in the middle depths
or near the surface. Few creatures live in the deepest depths
because it is too dark and too cold there.

The hammerhead shark has its eyes and nostrils far apart,
one at each end of its long, flat head. This allows it
to see in all directions and helps it smell food from far away.

Bottlenose dolphins swim in groups
called schools. They "talk" to each other
by making whistling, chirping,
clicking, and moaning sounds.

The leatherback turtle lives in warm seas.
It is the largest of all sea turtles. Its long, leathery
shell and powerful flippers help it swim
swiftly and easily through the water.

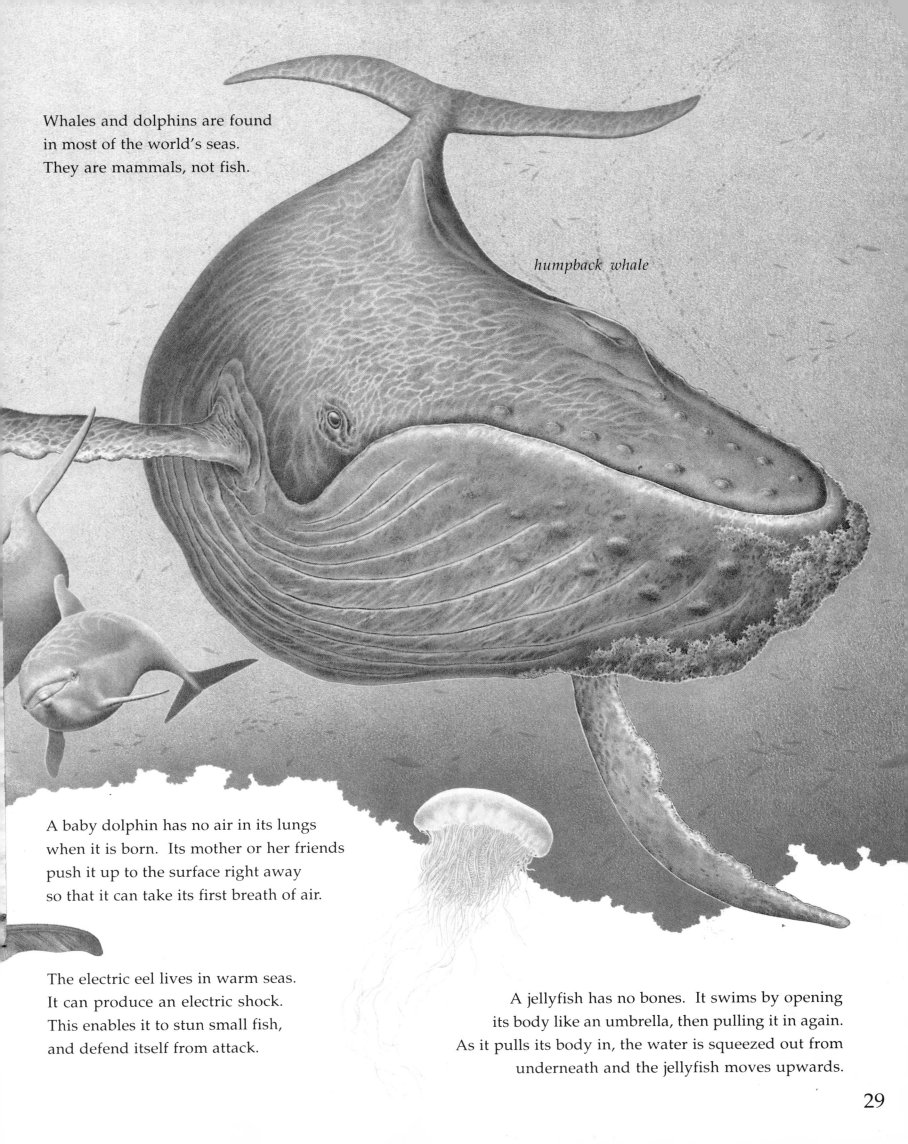

Whales and dolphins are found
in most of the world's seas.
They are mammals, not fish.

humpback whale

A baby dolphin has no air in its lungs
when it is born. Its mother or her friends
push it up to the surface right away
so that it can take its first breath of air.

The electric eel lives in warm seas.
It can produce an electric shock.
This enables it to stun small fish,
and defend itself from attack.

A jellyfish has no bones. It swims by opening
its body like an umbrella, then pulling it in again.
As it pulls its body in, the water is squeezed out from
underneath and the jellyfish moves upwards.

29

The Antarctic

The Antarctic is one of the coldest and windiest places on Earth. Most of the land is covered with thick ice all year round. Winter can last for nine months. Yet, in spite of these conditions, animals do live in the Antarctic, mainly around the coast. The seas are full of life and provide plenty of food.

To save energy, albatrosses flap their wings as little as possible. Instead, they glide on currents of wind—sometimes at speeds of up to 60 mph (96km/h).

Penguins have wings but cannot fly. Instead, they use their wings for swimming underwater. On land they either waddle clumsily or skid across the ice on their chests, pushing themselves forward with their wings and feet.

Elephant seals come ashore to breed in the spring. The males arrive first and fight with each other for their places on the beach.

Male elephant seals roar to frighten away rivals. Their long noses, when blown up, act like echo chambers and make their roaring sound very loud.

114